Also by Danielle Coke Balfour

A Heart on Fire: 100 Meditations on Loving Your Neighbors Well

A HEART ON FIRE

100 Activities and Prompts for a Life of Everyday Advocacy and Self-Compassion

DANIELLE COKE BALFOUR

Andrews McMeel
PUBLISHING®

"Do the work!"
"Take action!"
"Be the change!"

If you care about justice, empathy, and advocacy, you're no stranger to these declarations. It's true: to see meaningful transformation in society and an end to the injustices that are prevalent all around us, we must be active participants in building a more just and equitable world. Even so, this work is often easier said than done. We know that we each have a specific role to step into, but how exactly do we make it happen? Where do we start?

A Heart on Fire Guided Workbook seeks to serve as one of many answers to these pressing questions. Within these pages, you'll find 100 activities that will guide you through reflecting on, processing through, and planning out your unique contribution to the causes that matter most to you. From Venn diagrams and charts to coloring pages and illustrated prompts, this workbook will become your new companion as you journey through discovering your present purpose and building a life that boldly exemplifies the values that you hold dear.

If you're looking to go deeper, fortify your foundation, and practically apply your knowledge to a life of everyday advocacy, you've picked up the right workbook. If you're able, set aside about fifteen to twenty minutes each day to fully dive into each activity and the corresponding reflection questions that will follow. With each day that passes, you'll become clearer about your impact and more confident than ever that the world needs you and all of the good you bring.

TABLE OF

CONTENTS

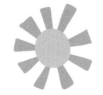

WHAT MY HEART HOLDS

Let's take inventory of your heart. In the spaces below, reflect on the provided prompts and write down all that comes to mind. When you're finished, you'll have a bird's-eye view of all that you hold dear and what matters most to you.

PEOPLE I LOVE:

WHAT I LOVE:

PLACES I LOVE:

HOW I LOVE:

How would you define love, personally? What does love mean to you?

How do you like to receive love? What actions or words make you feel loved?

When considering how to show love to someone else, why is it necessary to factor in the other person's wants and needs before taking action on their behalf?

LET'S

REFLECT

How can you practice intentionality when it comes to showing love to people in your life?

A LOVE THAT'S MORE THAN WORDS

Love is alive, taking on many forms and functions. We demonstrate it through the ways we check in with each other, tell the truth, and fight for each other's rights. In the hearts below, write examples of ways that we demonstrate care and concern for each other beyond simply saying "I love you."

EX: SPEAKING UP
WHEN WITNESSING
SOMEONE BEING
MISTREATED

Are there people in your life who consistently help others feel loved, worthy, and seen? Who are they?

Reflect on a time when you witnessed someone going out of their way to make someone else feel seen. What did you take away from that experience?

YEAR-ROUND VALENTINES

In the spaces below, think of people that you'd like to commit to loving unconditionally. Then, write out that commitment like it's a valentine you'd be giving them. Try to list out concrete ways that you'll show up for, care for, and stand up for them.

DEAR _____ ,

DEAR _____ ,

DEAR _____,

DEAR _____,

After writing out your commitments, reflect on ways that you can share these valentines with the people you wrote them about. This could be giving them a letter, having a conversation with them, or doing this activity with each other. If you'd prefer not to share the commitments with them directly, you can simply begin or continue living out these commitments in your life every day.

COME TOGETHER CROSSWORD

There are so many opportunities, big and small, to give back each day. This crossword puzzle activity covers fifteen different ways that we can come together and make a difference, both locally and globally!

Across

1. The repurposing and reprocessing of waste into new products; an alternative to throwing something away as trash
7. If you like what you bought, leaving a positive _____ can help the business owner tremendously
8. One way to give back is to support a local nonprofit _____ with funds, time, or spreading the word about the work they do
9. The city, town, or neighborhood that you live in; a social group that you belong to
10. "I love that outfit, you look amazing!"
11. Before dropping off a _____, make sure that you check out that organization's list of most-needed items and their guidelines for drop-offs
13. Eco-friendly and sustainable alternative to fast fashion or buying new
14. You can find animals who need a home here

Down

2. The act of freely giving away time, money, items, etc.; willingness to help in a way that goes above and beyond the norm
3. Make someone's day by leaving a kind, handwritten _____ somewhere where they can find it
4. When you join one of these, you pick a day and time where you'll prepare and/or deliver breakfast, lunch, or dinner for someone who could use the extra help in a busy or difficult season
5. You'll want many people to sign this when you want to bring about specific change for an important cause
6. Giving of your time to help others, often without monetary compensation
12. Working with a student to provide one-on-one academic support
14. _____ Business Saturday happens betwen Black Friday and Cyber Monday

MY GOOD DEED PLANNER

WHOM I WANT TO HELP AND WHY:

FINAL IDEA:

DATE AND TIME TO MAKE IT HAPPEN:

IDEA BRAIN DUMP:

SUPPLIES I'LL NEED:

WILL I NEED HELP?   YES   NO

NOTES:

Research the benefits of good deeds (for both the giver and the recipient) and write them below. Did any of these surprise you?

What are two ways that you can creatively show others that you appreciate them within the next few weeks?

SPEAKING TRUTH OVER YOURSELF

A lie you've believed
about yourself:

1 EX: I AM INVISIBLE

2

3

4

5

A truth to speak
over yourself:

1 EX: WHILE MY CIRCUMSTANCES
MAY CREATE FEELINGS OF
ISOLATION AND LONELINESS,
I AM NOT ALONE.

2

3

4

5

Are any of the the truths that you wrote down on the previous page difficult to believe? If yes, which one(s) and why?

Have you ever received a compliment that was hard to accept? What was it? Can you see the truth in it, even if you're not ready to fully believe it?

WHAT'S WITHIN MY REACH

As you cultivate a life of justice, empathy, and love, you will embody the values that matter most to you—yet these values won't always be shared by the people around you. Remember: while we seek to educate and empower others into adopting new perspectives, their actions and beliefs are ultimately out of our control. In this activity, you'll be able to differentiate between the work that is yours to do and the work that does not belong to you. Making this distinction will help you keep your main focus on living out the values that you hold dear.

THINGS OUT OF YOUR REACH   Ex: The past, lost time

THINGS WITHIN YOUR REACH   Ex: Your contribution to the world

Recall a time where you tried to change someone else's perspective and were unsuccessful. What did you take away from that experience?

How can focusing on what's within your reach have a positive impact on the people around you?

KEEPING MY OWN CUP FULL

When pouring out your life for others, it's increasingly important to have tried and true ways to fill your own cup too. Fill the cup below with all of your favorite ways to find restoration, inspiration, and enjoyment.

How can you safeguard and prioritize refilling your cup when your schedule gets busy?

What are the benefits of having regular rhythms of rest and renewal?

A LOVE LETTER TO MYSELF

DEAR _____ ,

P.S. YOU ARE SO LOVED!

Is there a piece of advice you often share with others that is difficult to internalize for yourself? If so, what is it and why?

LET'S REFLECT

Which direction are you more likely to lean: selflessness to the point of neglecting yourself, or self-centeredness to the point of only considering yourself? What small steps can you take to course-correct?

CREAT

MY SKILLS:

CAUSES I
CARE ABOUT:

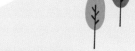

PRESENT
PURPOSE

MY PASSIONS:

MY PRESENT PURPOSE STATEMENT

Your present purpose can be found at the intersection of your skills, passions, and causes that you care about. Living out your present purpose simply means that you're taking action by combining the magic of those three categories and discovering something you can do right here and now for the issues that matter to you. Brainstorm your skills, passions, and causes on page 24, then use the templates below to craft your own present purpose statements by combining one skill, one passion, and one cause to create an action plan.

I WILL USE MY SKILL OF _____
(SKILL)

AND MY PASSION FOR _____ TO
(PASSION)

_____ FOR MY
(ACTION)

_____
(COMMUNITY YOU'RE SERVING)

AS I WORK TO FIGHT FOR _____ .
(CAUSE OR ISSUE)

I WILL USE MY SKILL OF _____
(SKILL)

AND MY PASSION FOR _____ TO
(PASSION)

_____ FOR MY
(ACTION)

_____
(COMMUNITY YOU'RE SERVING)

AS I WORK TO FIGHT FOR _____ .
(CAUSE OR ISSUE)

HOW I EXPRESS CREATIVITY

The concept of creativity is often reserved for traditional artists, but each of us is creative by nature. Think of your daily life and name five things that you make everyday. For example, do you make a cup of coffee? Do you make a morning commute to work? Brainstorm in the space below.

Each day, you have an opportunity to exercise creativity. Take a few of your answers above and come up with ways to do something new, unique, or fun with them. For example, could you try a new brand of coffee creamer or switch up your morning commute?

Problem-solving is another way to be creative. Is there something in your life that could be improved through a fresh and creative point of view? This could be anything from a new idea for tackling family chores to proposing a helpful concept at your next company meeting.

Is there a passion project or creative outlet that you've wanted to try? What is it, and how can you take one step toward making it happen in the weeks ahead?

I AM NOT WHAT I DO

In a society obsessed with productivity, it's easy to feel like your worth and value are tied to your output. In the slice of the pie chart below, write down what you do for a living, your hobbies, or what you're known for. In the green section of the chart, write down your qualities, values, encouraging ways that others have described you, or positive things that you see in yourself. In the end, you'll be able to view yourself as so much more than your accomplishments.

WHO I AM:

WHAT I DO:

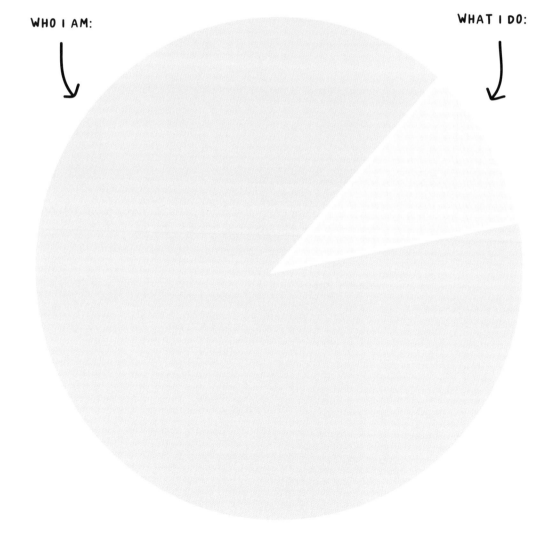

Have you struggled with finding your identity in what you do? How can you create or maintain a healthy separation between who you are and what you do?

How do you normally handle criticism? How can you reframe the negative self-talk that can arise after receiving feedback?

THE ART OF THE IN—BETWEEN

In life, we're consistently taught that masterpieces have to be finished products. Many of us have unfinished projects or dormant ideas that are waiting to be revived. In the frame below, write down any paused dreams or incomplete works, and then draw and color in around them using whatever tools you'd like. You can use symbols, draw pictures, write your ideas in bold letters, doodle random shapes, etc. Let's turn those in-between works into a finished masterpiece, right here.

Do you struggle with the in-between seasons? Why or why not?

In what ways can you enjoy the journey and celebrate your progress in different areas of your life?

TURNING A NEW PAGE

A NEW PERSPECTIVE I CAN ADOPT:

A NEW WAY I CAN GIVE MYSELF ROOM TO BREATHE:

A NEW IDEA I WANT TO BRAINSTORM ABOUT:

Do you normally reserve fresh starts for the new year? How can you make room for fresh starts throughout the year?

Do you give yourself blank space during your day? These could be moments of quiet, room to breathe, margin for error, etc. If not, how can you start?

WORD SEARCH SOUP

These words represent some of the many attributes that make up your unique contribution to the world. See if you can find them all!

```
N K Z X P G G X T K N G E V B V U L U
Z O V R N K U J V V J T D O R E O I E
M W I F U S S P I A T Y R I J X Z P Q
T A L E N T S K H F J J X C I U P A I
L Z T S U R I Q Z R B M P E S Z E S R
D R X C O M M U N I T Y U H B T G S J
M V I S I O N P V N L L V K K S W I P
G W G A H X V C J G Y D W X O M L O N
U H O S W C J O U Q J N C S V G I N R
E J R T G P D R S C U L T U R E L S S
I Q A Y V N J G T E V Q A V G L U R Q
V Q S L Y Z K W O U J L B I L W E F W
D H I E D F K D R I Z N M S O X E K I
N A O M T P B Q Y W O E E Z K T P V A
O C T B N U J E T I H P V U D I Q G Q
R U J T B B C B Z A J L U W X X L A P
L J Z P S I S M Q A R Q A F Y I U L M
P D H Z V M E P Y M R O B D F S L Q S
Z D X B P P R S M Y F X L T N T L L Y
```

COMMUNITY   PASSIONS   CULTURE   SKILLS   STORY
TALENTS   HOBBIES   VISION   STYLE   VOICE

Your passions, culture, skills, style, community, and more all combine to tell your story. This is completely unique to you. What is your story? How did you get to where you are today, and how does your story enable you to show up for others in your own way?

LET'S REFLECT

MY LITTLE IS MORE THAN ENOUGH

Have you ever struggled with feeling like your contribution to the world is insignificant? Why or why not?

There are actions that may seem small on their own, but when done by many people, they can have a monumental impact on the world. List a few examples of these kinds of actions.

There are people in your orbit that you can impact in ways that no one else can. List five people below whom you do life with and describe your relationship with them. In what ways can you influence them for good?

Write down three influential people in history who changed the world with a single action, gift, or skill and reflect on their impact.

HIDDEN GEMS FOUND IN CHAOS

When unexpected trouble arises, it can be quite challenging to spot the good moments in the midst of so much difficulty. In this activity, you'll have an opportunity to look back at a stressful or chaotic situation that you've lived through and spot the lessons that you were able to pull from it in its aftermath.

MY TORNADO OF TROUBLE WAS:

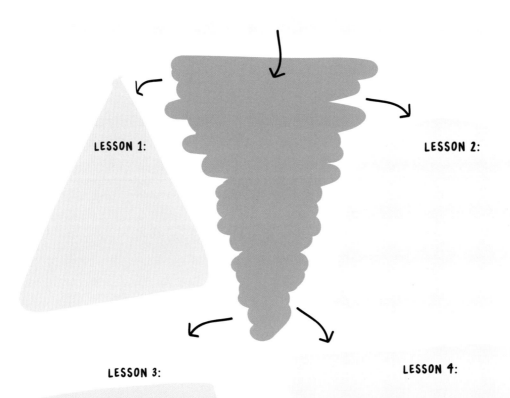

LESSON 1:

LESSON 2:

LESSON 3:

LESSON 4:

It's been said that creativity thrives in constraint. Has this been true for you before? In what ways have you been motivated by having limited time, resources, or support?

When difficult situations show up in your life, what are your strategies for staying afloat?

THE BUILDING BLOCKS OF CHANGEMAKING

What's a broken system that you believe needs to be dismantled or completely reformed? Describe it. This can be something you've witnessed on a state or national level, or something you've witnessed in your personal life, like a toxic system or an abusive organization.

What steps can be taken to dismantle or reform this system? What role can you play in this process, if possible?

Imagine a new or equitable way forward for this system or organization. How would this new future feel? What would be your goals? How would change be measured?

In a practical sense, how can things be restructured or shifted to end the cycle of harm, toxicity, or abuse in this system or organization?

Has perfectionism ever shown up in your life or activism? How does it affect your ability to do what you're called to do?

LET'S

REFLECT

What are the benefits of embracing your imperfections?

MY GOOD WORK GLOSSARY

When living a life of justice and good work, you'll come across many terms that are important to define and understand. You may have a general idea of what some or all of these terms mean, but getting specific with definitions increases your confidence in the subject matter and allows you to spot when meanings are being twisted or redefined. This exercise will give you space to research definitions of commonly used terms in justice-focused conversations. You'll also be able to make those definitions personal to you by choosing a quote that contains that term and embodies its definition.

JUSTICE

Definition:

Quote:

One synonym:
One antonym:

EQUITY

Definition:

Quote:

One synonym:
One antonym:

DIVERSITY

Definition:

Quote:

One synonym:
One antonym:

DIGNITY

Definition:

Quote:

One synonym:
One antonym:

LIBERATION

Definition:

Quote:

One synonym:
One antonym:

PRIVILEGE

Definition:

Quote:

One synonym:
One antonym:

OPPRESSION

Definition:

Quote:

One synonym:
One antonym:

EQUALITY

Definition:

Quote:

One synonym:
One antonym:

ADVOCACY

Definition:

Quote:

One synonym:
One antonym:

INCLUSION

Definition:

Quote:

One synonym:
One antonym:

ILLUMINATING PRIVILEGE

Privilege is a form of advantage that you're given based on certain attributes that you have. It takes many forms and is often wielded to the detriment of entire people groups. In this activity, you'll have an opportunity to identify certain privileges that you may possess and reflect on ways that you can use your privilege for good in the world around you.

LIST EXAMPLES OF PRIVILEGE HERE:

A privilege that I have:

How I benefit from it:

How I can use my privilege for good:

A privilege that I have: _____

How I benefit from it:

How I can use my privilege for good:

A privilege that I have: _____

How I benefit from it:

How I can use my privilege for good:

A privilege that I have: _____

How I benefit from it:

How I can use my privilege for good:

FIGHTING MARGINALIZATION

Injustice in society thrives on certain communities consistently being mariginalized and excluded. Justice involves righting these wrongs through implementing policies and reforming systems, as well as taking personal responsibility to amplify, protect, and fight for these communities in our own daily lives. Choose two historically excluded communities that you seek to begin or continue advocating for in your daily life and highlight both indiviudal and systemic changes that can be taken to fight marginalization.

Historically excluded community:

Policy changes that can improve societal conditions for this community:

Ways that I can personally advocate for this community:

Historically excluded community:

Policy changes that can improve societal conditions for this community:

Ways that I can personally advocate for this community:

Pick one community that you wrote about and research a proposed bill or piece of legislation that has been proposed to **improve** societal conditions for this group. What is it and how would you explain its goal?

LET'S REFLECT

Pick one community that you wrote about and research a proposed bill or piece of legislation that has been proposed that could potentially **worsen** societal conditions for this group. What is it and how would you explain its goal?

ANALYZING ROOT CAUSES

While we work to treat the symptoms of broken systems in society, we must also do the work of investigating root causes. In this activity, identify ways that we can treat the fruit of harmful systems while also working to uproot them.

WE CAN TREAT THE FRUIT BY:

Ex: Donating food to food banks

FOOD INSECURITY

WE CAN UPROOT IT BY:

Ex: Providing living wages

WE CAN TREAT THE FRUIT BY:

EDUCATION DISPARITIES

WE CAN UPROOT IT BY:

WE CAN TREAT THE FRUIT BY: WE CAN UPROOT IT BY:

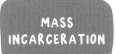

MASS
INCARCERATION

WE CAN TREAT THE FRUIT BY: HOMELESSNESS   WE CAN UPROOT IT BY:

PROCESSING COLLECTIVE HEARTBREAK

Is there a headline, national tragedy, or global issue that's weighing on your heart right now? What is it?

What emotions are you currently experiencing? Write out as much as you can.

One way to move through collective heartbreak is finding a way to mobilize. What is one small way you can give, amplify, or use your voice?

What are glimmers of hope that can be found in the midst of the heartbreak? Think of stories of people coming together, organizations doing good work on the ground, etc.

What's one way that you can use your gift to process through this heartbreak and bring light to the world?

Whom in your community can you trust to hold your honest thoughts and questions about this topic right now?

MEASURING EQUITY EFFORTS

In an effort to practice transparency concerning diversity, equity, and inclusion efforts, many corporations and organizations release annual diversity reports. For this activity, you'll get to choose one company, review their most recent diversity report (bonus points if this is is a company that you already support), and reflect on the way they measure progress.

CHOSEN COMPANY TO REVIEW:

DEMOGRAPHIC DATA OR DIVERSITY STATISTICS:

TITLE AND PAGE LENGTH OF DEI REPORT:

ONE NOTABLE EXAMPLE OF PROGRESS:

DIVERSITY OF THE C-SUITE:

ONE GOAL THEY HAVE FOR THE FUTURE:

COMMUNITY IMPACT:

What else stood out to you about this diversity report? Do you think that this company is making meaningful progress in this area? Why or why not?

LET'S

REFLECT

What are other ways that companies could improve their DEI efforts?

MICROAGGRESSIVE GREETING CARDS

Microaggressions are verbal or behavioral slights, often intended as compliments, that reinforce stereotypes or negative beliefs about historically excluded communities. Use the blank cards below to create your own microaggressive greeting cards. These can be microaggressions that you've been on the receiving end of, ones you've heard said to others, or ones you've said yourself.

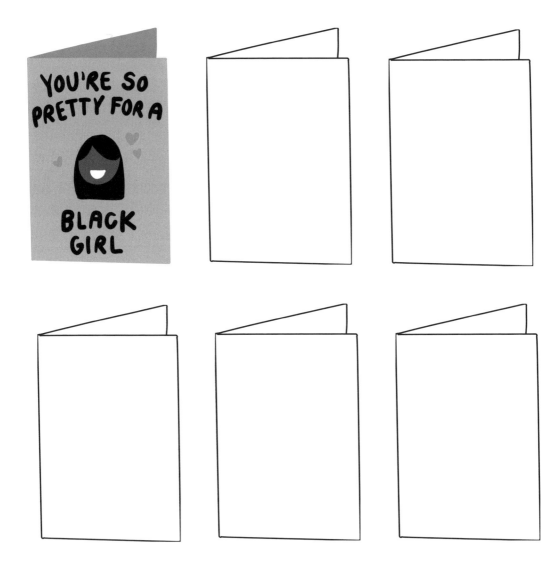

Have you ever been on the receiving end of a microaggression? What was it, and how did you respond? What did you take away from that experience?

Have you ever been guilty of a microaggression? What was it, and how did the recipient respond? What did you take away from that experience?

What are the benefits of diversity?

How can you tell the difference between performative and authentic efforts to diversify?

SEEDS OF CHANGE

When working for justice, it's crucial to pause and take in the ways we've achieved progress. This helps us resist despondency, reminds us that better is possible, and encourages us to keep moving forward with hope. Use this activity to reflect on improvements we've made as a society in any area that matters to you.

IMPROVEMENT 1: _____

IMPROVEMENT 2: _____

IMPROVEMENT 3: _____

How do you keep yourself reminded of the good in the world when we're consistently experiencing so much injustice?

Why is it important to keep seeking joy and reading good news, especially in difficult seasons?

MAKING ROOM FOR HEALING

Seeking justice takes a toll on our hearts, minds, and bodies. Below each vase, write a word that represents what you want to make more room for in your life as your pursue continuous healing and restoration. Then, draw flowers in that vase to represent how incorporating this word into your life can help you grow, heal, and experience more beauty.

JOY

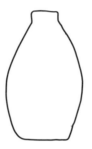

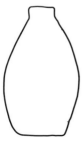

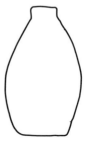

How can you take steps to incorporate your chosen words into your daily life?

How does embarking on a healing journey impact your justice efforts?

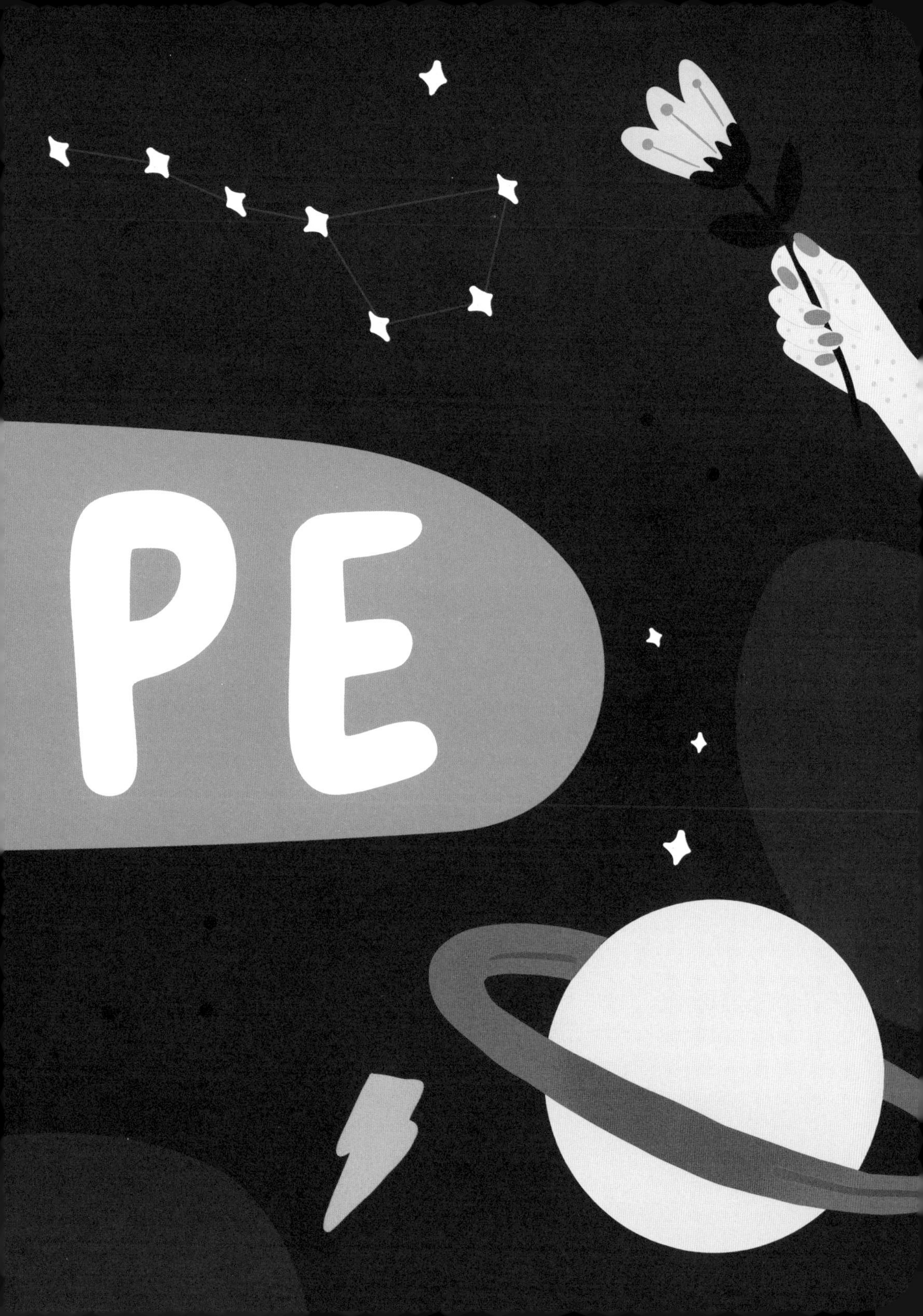
PE

MY STORM SURVIVAL KIT

Life's challenges can easily catch us off guard and foil our best-laid plans. We can't always see them coming, but we can put systems and practices in place to make sure that we can access encouragement, hope, and connection during those storms. In this activity, you'll have a chance to identify ways that you can anticipate your own needs and care for yourself well during difficult seasons.

QUOTES OR TRUTHS
I CAN CLING TO:

PEOPLE I CAN
CALL OR LEAN ON:

WAYS I CAN
CARE FOR MYSELF:

HOW I WILL SHOW
MYSELF GRACE:

It's been said that storms often turn us into softer, kinder, and more empathetic people. Is this true for you? Describe an example of this.

LET'S
REFLECT

If you could write a page of a storm survival guide for someone else, what hopeful reminders would you give them?

HOPE IN THE WAITING

Are you in a season of waiting? What are you currently waiting on or hoping for?

How has this season of waiting been for you? What emotions have you been experiencing?

How have you been coping with your season? Do you have any practices or strategies?

Part of hope involves grieving and holding the weight of your unmet expectations or change of plans. What are you grieving? How have you given yourself space to move through this grief?

How can you practice gratitude, even here in the waiting?

Where are you finding hope right now?

MY WINDSHIELD AND REARVIEW

In difficult seasons, we can find encouragement and motivation from looking back and reflecting on times where we've climbed mountains and overcame challenging circumstances. Like a rearview mirror, our past can inform our future, but what's ahead of us is where our main focus shoud lie. In this activity, let's reflect on a few of our past victories and let that inspire our future hopes and dreams.

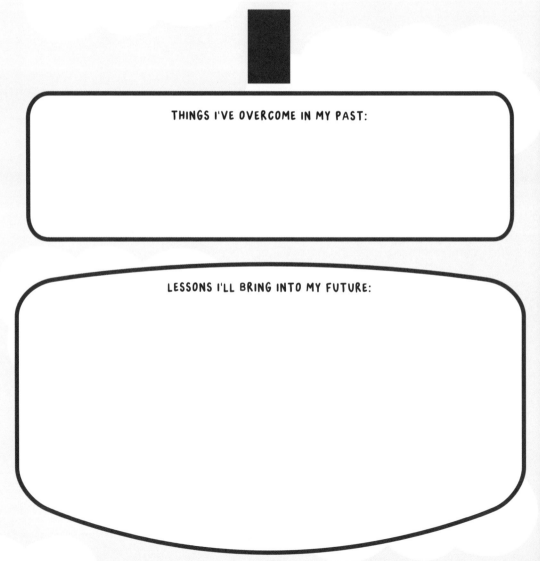

THINGS I'VE OVERCOME IN MY PAST:

LESSONS I'LL BRING INTO MY FUTURE:

Why is focusing on the present and future more important than focusing on the past?

How would you compare who you are today to who you were five years ago? What's changed? What's stayed the same?

HOPE FROM OUR HEROES

One encouraging reality about history is that we can often find hope from tho who have come before us. In this activity, you'll be able to identify historica figures whom you're inspired by, reflect on some of the obstacles they endur and draw inspiration from the way they navigated those obstacles.

An obstacle they overcame:

MY HERO'S NAME IS:

A quote from them that gives me hope:

An obstacle they overcame:

MY HERO'S NAME IS:

A quote from them that gives me hope:

An obstacle they overcame:

MY HERO'S NAME IS:

A quote from them that gives me hope:

MY HERO'S NAME IS:

An obstacle they overcame:

A quote from them that gives me hope:

PLANT YOUR DREAMS AND WATCH THEM GROW

SOME OF MY HOPES AND DREAMS:

 ONE DREAM I'M FOCUSING ON:

LOVED ONES I CAN LEAN ON FOR SUPPORT AS I PLANT THIS DREAM:

WAYS I'LL GAIN KNOWLEDGE ABOUT MY DREAM:

PEOPLE, PLACES, OR THINGS THAT INSPIRE ME TO PURSUE MY DREAM:

DOUBTS AND FEARS TO CUT AWAY:

TOOLS I'LL NEED:

What has held you back from pursuing your dreams in the past?

LET'S

REFLECT

Write down three affirmations that you can use to remind yourself that you're capable of chasing after your dreams.

EX: I BELIEVE THAT I WAS MADE FOR THIS MOMENT AND PUT ON EARTH TO DO THIS.

SONGS OF FREEDOM

Even in the most dire circumstances, people throughout history were determined to cling to the hope of finding freedom. In history, enslaved people were known to keep the faith through songs and spirituals as they dreamt of making their escapes to freedom. These kinds of songs also encouraged and empowered Black people throughout the civil rights movement. Unscramble the words in the activity below to reveal specific titles of these songs of liberation.

GSINW OLW TSEWE CHOTRIA

_____

WLFOLO TEH INDKNRGI GDOUR

_____

EWAD NI HET EATRW

_____

LEATS AWYA

_____

OG WDON ESMSO

_____

EW LAHSL ECMEVROO

_____

HO RMEDOEF

_____

WDNO YB THE RSREEDIIV

_____

OHW I TOG VROE

_____

Pick a freedom song from this activity and write the lyrics down below. What sticks out to you?

How do chants, spirituals, and songs of liberation catalyze or maintain a movement?

HOPES FULFILLED

One way to keep hope alive is to remember those moments when your hopes were fulfilled. In this activity, reflect on three moments when something that you were working toward, dreaming of, or hoping for came to pass.

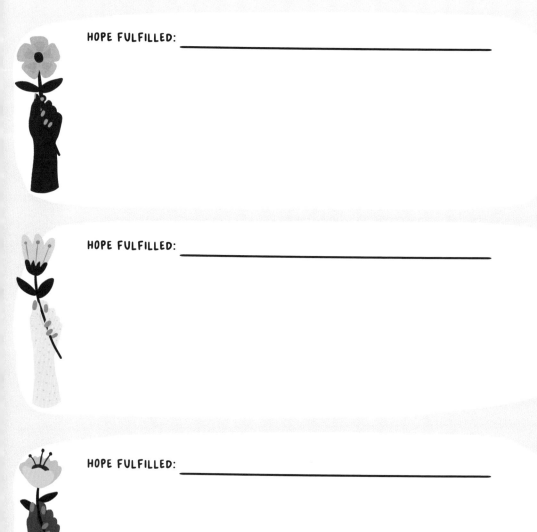

HOPE FULFILLED: _____

HOPE FULFILLED: _____

HOPE FULFILLED: _____

Did looking back on your fulfilled hopes encourage you? Why or why not?

LET'S

REFLECT

How can you remind yourself of those moments when your dreams came to pass? You could print out photos to keep on your fridge, frame your diploma, journal about it, etc.

PRACTICING CONSCIOUS OPTIMISM

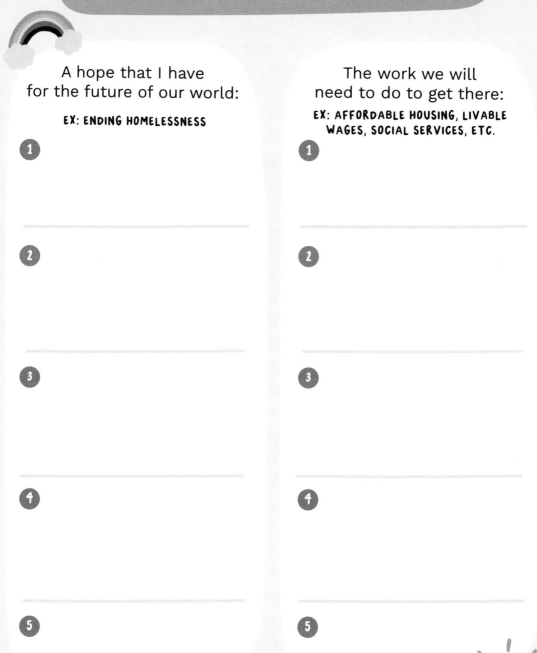

A hope that I have for the future of our world:

EX: ENDING HOMELESSNESS

1

2

3

4

5

The work we will need to do to get there:

EX: AFFORDABLE HOUSING, LIVABLE WAGES, SOCIAL SERVICES, ETC.

1

2

3

4

5

Choose one of your hopes from this activity and brainstorm a way that you can contribute to seeing this hope fulfilled.

LET'S REFLECT

When it comes to the future of society and achieving these hopes, would you consider yourself optimistic, pessimistic, or realistic? Why or why not? What role does hope play in your worldview?

A CANDLE OF HOPE

When encouraging someone else, it's important to choose language that doesn't invalidate their feelings or overwhelm them with toxic positivity. In this activity, you'll get to brainstorm gentle and helpful phrases to use when attempting to encourage others during moments of difficulty.

PHRASES TO SOLIDIFY YOUR PRESENCE

Ex: "I'm here for you."

PHRASES TO VALIDATE THEIR EMOTIONS

Ex: "You have a right to feel that way."

PHRASES THAT ACKNOWLEDGE THE DIFFICULTY OF THE SITUATION OR SEASON

Ex: "This is so hard."

PHRASES THAT EXPRESS A DESIRE TO HOLD SPACE

Ex: "I'm here for you."

What are examples of unhelpful or discouraging words that you've received during seasons of difficulty?

LET'S REFLECT

What are examples of helpful or encouraging words that you've received during seasons of difficulty?

TEN TRUTHS TO CLING TO

On the sticky notes across these two pages, write out ten reminders to yourself that you can refer back to on hard days. These can be quotes, scriptures, personal mottos, single words, pieces of advice, or anything else that will help you keep going when the journey gets weary. This is one of many ways to cling to hope each day.

WHEN HOPE FEELS DISTANT

When you're finished, consider transferring a few of these quotes onto real sticky notes and placing them in areas that your eyes will be drawn to throughout your days. A few ideas include your bathroom mirror, fridge, work computer, or journal! You could also write a few inspiring messages for others on sticky notes and leave them where they can find them.

ALL ABOUT THAT TOPIC!

A WAR

SOLIDIFYING WHAT YOU STAND FOR

One of the first steps in cultivating awareness of the role we play in justice efforts involves having a strong sense of your core values and beliefs. Use the following prompts as a guide to work through discovering what matters most to you and how having an awareness of these beliefs can inform your changemaking efforts.

WHAT ARE MY CORE BELIEFS?

WHAT ABOUT SOCIETY ANNOYS OR IRRITATES ME?

HOW HAVE I BEEN SHAPED BY MAJOR LIFE EXPERIENCES?

WHAT MAKES MY HEART COME ALIVE?

HOW DO I WANT TO BE REMEMBERED WHEN I'M GONE?

Based on your answers on the previous page, how would you summarize what you stand for?

LET'S

REFLECT

How do you demonstrate your values in your daily life?

MY CHANGEMAKING ROLE

What are some issues or causes that you can educate others about? This can be a cause that you know a lot about and/or have context with through lived experience.

What are some issues or causes that you don't have a lot of context or knowledge on but have wanted to learn more about?

What are practical ways that you can amplify the voice of someone else who has context or lived experience regarding a specific issue?

Reflect on a mistake that you made on your changemaking journey. What happened, and what did you take away from it?

If someone you know wanted to get involved in changemaking and giving back, how would you encourage them? What advice or first steps would you give them?

PASSING THE MICROPHONE

From board rooms to doctors' offices, there are countless moments where voices that deserve to be heard are overlooked. Each of us has the power to speak up on behalf of historically excluded communities in our daily life. Whom can you speak up or advocate for? This can be a specific person or a group of people. Use this activity to process through ways that you can start (or continue) amplifying the voices of others. For example, is there a coworker whom you notice is always being spoken over in meetings? Or are you passionate about foster care and protecting vulnerable children? Brainstorm your own examples below.

PERSON OR GROUP: _____

HOW I CAN AMPLIFY THEIR VOICE(S):

PERSON OR GROUP: _____

HOW I CAN AMPLIFY THEIR VOICE(S):

PERSON OR GROUP: _____

HOW I CAN AMPLIFY THEIR VOICE(S):

Reflect on a time where someone else advocated for you or amplified your voice. What happened and how did it affect you?

How can you ensure that you're centering the experiences of historically excluded communities while advocating for them?

NARROWING DOWN YOUR ACTION

Let's take a deep dive into a social issue you've been wanting to learn more about and move through the information-to-action funnel below. Start by identifying the issue, choosing sources, and conducting a few minutes of research. At the end, you'll have a new idea for a single action you can take to make a difference for a cause that you care about.

GENERAL KNOWLEDGE

MY CHOSEN ISSUE: _____

CHOOSING SOURCES

SOURCE 1 _____

SOURCE 2 _____

SOURCE 3 _____

SPEND SOME TIME WITH THESE
SOURCES AND TAKE NOTES BELOW:
↓

TOPICAL RESEARCH

WHAT STOOD OUT
TO YOU? WHAT IS
STIRRING YOUR
HEART?

PAIRING PASSION WITH A CAUSE

NAME TWO ORGANIZATIONS
THAT DO GOOD WORK WITH
THIS TOPIC:

NAME TWO WAYS THAT
YOU CAN SUPPORT THE CAUSE
USING YOUR PASSIONS:

CHOOSE ONE
↓

ALIGNED ACTION

ONE ACTION YOU WILL TAKE IN
SUPPORT OF THIS CAUSE:

What is your learning style? Do you prefer visual imagery, using your hands, having conversations, reading, or other formats?

Has learning about social issues ever been overwhelming for you? If so, in what ways? Have you ever experienced information overload?

How can you create rhythms of learning about the causes that matter to you in ways that align with your learning styles?

THE JOURNEY OF LIFELONG LEARNING

Reflect on how much you've grown during this past season of your life. Which lessons will you forever cling to?

Write about a mistake that helped you chart a new way forward and make a change in your life.

Recall a time where you received new information that challenged what you thought you knew about a specific issue or subject. How did that transform your journey?

How has community shaped your journey of lifelong learning? How do you involve your loved ones in your discovery, course correction, and action?

Reflect on a time where you were called in and held accountable. How did that experience shape you? How have you lived differently since that moment?

SEEING RACIAL DISPARITIES

While the phrase "I don't see color" is often well-intentioned, those who claim to live by this motto can easily live a life that's oblivious to the complexities of racial issues and the pervasive inequities that we still face as a society. In this activity, you'll be able to look into current racial disparities in multiple sectors and be reminded of the ongoing need to seek justice and eradicate racist systems.

NAME A RACIAL DISPARITY IN HEALTHCARE:

Ex: Black people are more likely to die from cancer than any other group.

NAME A RACIAL DISPARITY IN EDUCATION:

NAME A RACIAL DISPARITY IN EMPLOYMENT:

NAME A RACIAL DISPARITY IN HOUSING:

NAME A RACIAL DISPARITY
IN WEALTH:

NAME A RACIAL DISPARITY
IN INCARCERATION:

NAME A RACIAL DISPARITY
IN GOVERNMENT:

NAME A RACIAL DISPARITY
IN VOTING RIGHTS:

NAME A RACIAL DISPARITY
IN BANKING:

NAME A RACIAL DISPARITY IN

_____

(CHOOSE YOUR OWN)

If you were making protest signs to advocate for causes that you believe in, what would they say? Fill the protest signs on these pages with your own slogans, protest art, or both!

PICKING A CAUSE

If you're having trouble narrowing down a cause to support in this season, there are three places you can look: personal experiences, passions, and proximity. This activity will help you explore these areas and land on a cause that you can start (or continue) supporting today.

PERSONAL EXPERIENCES THAT DRAW ME TO CERTAIN CAUSES:

Ex: An illness that a family member battles

PASSIONS THAT DRAW ME TO CERTAIN CAUSES:

Ex: Being passionate about racial justice

PROXIMITY THAT DRAWS ME TO CERTAIN CAUSES:

Ex: Living in a city with polluted drinking water

MY TOP THREE CAUSES:

THE ONE CAUSE I'LL FOCUS ON THIS SEASON:

Why is it important for everyday people to engage in advocating for a cause that they believe in?

How can you get (or stay) connected to people who advocate for the same cause(s) that you care about?

WE WILL ALWAYS NEED EACH OTHER

ORGANIZATION INVESTIGATION

AN ORGANIZATION I
WANT TO SUPPORT:

WHO LEADS THE ORGANIZATION:

THE ORGANIZATION'S CHARITY RATING:

THREE WAYS THAT THIS
ORGANIZATION DOES GOOD WORK:

TWO WAYS I'D LIKE TO SUPPORT
THIS ORGANIZATION:

THIS ORGANIZATION'S VISION OR MISSION:

What factors help to determine whether or not you'll support an organization?

Not all impactful organizations are nonprofits. Identify a local mutual aid or grassroots movement that you could learn more about in the future and describe their vision or mission below.

COMM

UNITY

COLLECTIVE LIBERATION

There are issues that may seem unrelated on the surface but are connected and linked in many ways. In this activity, compare and contrast two existing social justice issues through research and find ways that they overlap with each other.

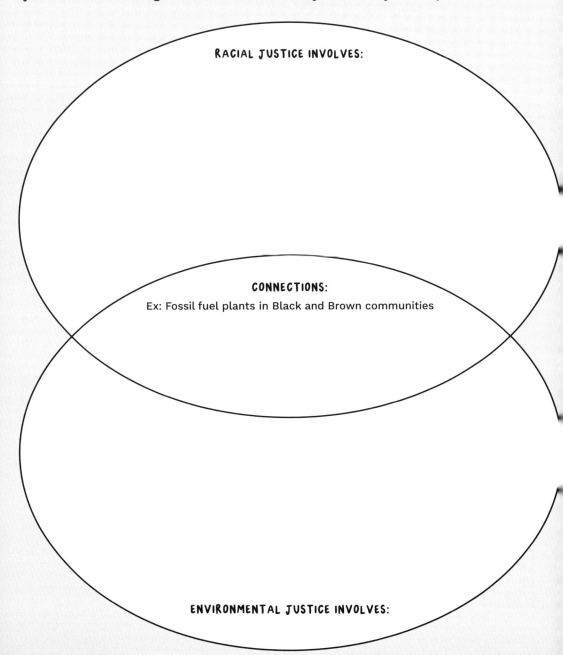

RACIAL JUSTICE INVOLVES:

CONNECTIONS:

Ex: Fossil fuel plants in Black and Brown communities

ENVIRONMENTAL JUSTICE INVOLVES:

Now it's your turn to choose! Fill out the diagram below with two issues that you believe are linked to each other and identify both their differences and connections. By the end of this activity, you'll have increased your ability to measure interconnectedness and how injustices are linked together.

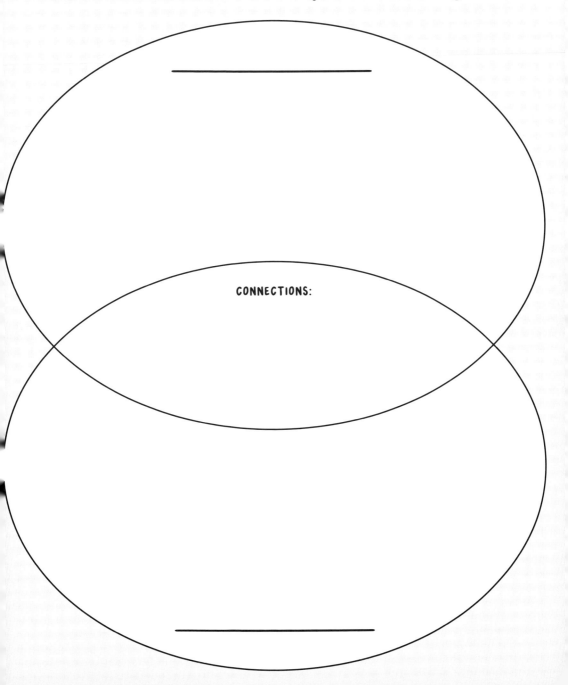

CONNECTIONS:

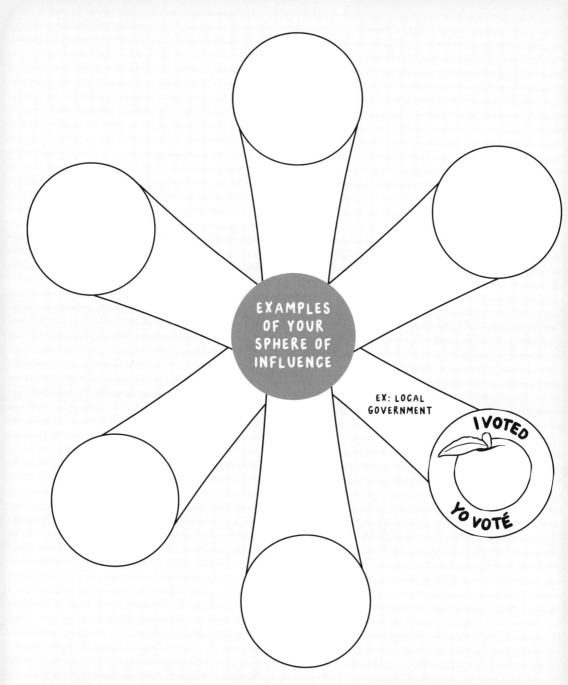

EXAMPLES OF YOUR SPHERE OF INFLUENCE

EX: LOCAL GOVERNMENT

I VOTED

YO VOTÉ

You have influence in the world around you in so many ways! Fill in the paths in the diagram above with places that you go to on a daily, weekly, monthly, or annual basis, while prioritizing the places where you go most often. In the corresponding circles you can draw an image that represents that place.

Next to each circle on the previous page, write an estimated number of people you may come into contact with when you're at that place. For example, if you listed your home as part of your sphere and you live with four people, put four. Then, add up all of those numbers and put the estimated total in the circle to the right.

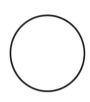

Are you surprised by the estimated total? Do you feel like you actually have influence on the people around you? Why or why not?

List ways that you can positively impact the people you encounter within your sphere of influence.

MY COMMUNITY

Whether you're surrounded by a loyal friend group you've known since college or are connected to one or two tried-and-true loved ones, it's important to cultivate a sense of care and connection with others. Fill in the blanks with the name(s) that come to mind after reading each description. You can repeat certain names if they fit more than one blank. When you complete the activity, you'll have a list of some of the people that you can count on as you journey through life.

I FEEL LOVED AND CARED FOR BY _____

I FEEL CELEBRATED BY _____

_____ MOTIVATE(S) AND INSPIRE(S) ME

WHEN I NEED TO GET MOVING ON AN IDEA, I CALL _____

_____ WILL ALWAYS TELL ME THE TRUTH

I CAN DREAM BIG WITH _____

I LOOK UP TO _____

I FEEL COMFORTED AND HEARD BY _____

MY SECRETS ARE SAFE WITH _____

I ALWAYS HAVE A FUN TIME WITH _____

Read the following descriptions and circle true or false based on which answer is true for you most of the time:

TRUE / FALSE   I TRY MY BEST TO CELEBRATE OTHERS WELL.

TRUE / FALSE   I KEEP OTHERS' SECRETS AS LONG AS IT'S SAFE TO DO SO.

TRUE / FALSE   I HOLD SPACE FOR OTHERS AND PRACTICE EMPATHY.

TRUE / FALSE   I TELL OTHERS THE TRUTH, EVEN IF IT MIGHT HURT.

TRUE / FALSE   I AM A SAFE PERSON TO DREAM WITH.

TRUE / FALSE   I PROVIDE MENTORSHIP OR ADVICE TO OTHERS.

TRUE / FALSE   I AM GENERALLY ENJOYABLE TO BE AROUND.

TRUE / FALSE   I BRAINSTORM WAYS TO SHOW PEOPLE THAT I LOVE THEM.

TRUE / FALSE   I TRY TO MOTIVATE AND INSPIRE OTHERS.

Based on your answers, how do you feel about the ways that you show up in your relationships? Is there anything that you'd like to adjust or do differently in your relationships in the future?

CULTIVATING COMMUNITY

Are you looking for ways to meet new people and expand your community? Check out the ideas included below for ways to step out with bravery to cultivate new relationships or revive existing ones. Circle the ones that interest you the most.

VOLUNTEERING

MAKING A LIST OF PEOPLE YOU WANT TO CHECK IN WITH

STAYING AFTER EVENTS TO STRIKE UP CONVERSATION

JOINING SOCIAL NETWORKING SITES

ATTENDING EVENTS SOLO

BEING FRIENDLY

GIVING COMPLIMENTS

SITTING AT COFFEE SHOPS

SIGNING UP TO TAKE A CLASS

Choose two ideas that you're willing to try out over the next few weeks or months and put them in the blanks below.

IDEA 1: _____

How can you activate or improve this daily practice?

IDEA 2: _____

How can you activate or improve this daily practice?

In the table below, list some of your passions or hobbies and then brainstorm an idea on how you can make or cultivate connections that align with that passion or hobby.

EX: BAKING	JOINING A CAKE DECORATING CLASS

Reflect on a time when you were hurt in community, and another time when you were healed and encouraged in community.

TRUE PEACE VS. FALSE PEACE

Have you ever experienced the awkward silence after an argument? Things may be calm, but we wouldn't necessarily describe the atmosphere as peaceful. Similarly, a sense of false peace shows up in numerous ways in society, as well as throughout history. In this activity, think through additional examples of true peace vs. false peace, whether in your personal life or throughout history.

FALSE PEACE LOOKS LIKE:

Ex: Black people quietly sitting in the back of a segregated bus

TRUE PEACE LOOKS LIKE:

Ex: Desegregated buses and the freedom to sit anywhere

FALSE PEACE LOOKS LIKE:

TRUE PEACE LOOKS LIKE:

FALSE PEACE LOOKS LIKE:

TRUE PEACE LOOKS LIKE:

Pursuing peace can sometimes involve stirring the pot. Reflect on a time in your life where you had to have a tough conversation with an end goal of true peace and restoration.

Why can it be harmful to settle for false peace?

REFLECTING ON WOMEN'S RIGHTS

History tells the story of a long struggle for equal rights and respect for women. What are some struggles that **all women** share in society today?

What are struggles that **women of color** in particular face in society today? Think of pay gaps, employment, beauty standards, etc.

What is misogynoir? How does misogynoir show up in society today?

How can we collectively do a better job at advocating for and protecting women in society today?

THE GIFT OF PRESENCE

There's nothing like the feeling of support and love that we feel when spending time with loved ones, especialy in seasons of difficulty. What are some benefits, or "gifts," that you receive when you're in the presence of your loved ones during tough times? Pick three and describe them in the spaces below.

GIFT 1: _____

GIFT 2: _____

GIFT 3: _____

Reflect on a time where someone came to spend time with you or invited you over in a difficult season. What was that experience like for you?

LET'S

REFLECT

In what ways do you try to show up and give the gift of presence to others when they're navigating challenging times? Whom can you spend time with this month and why?

FILL-IN-THE-BLANK MANIFESTO

IN THIS _____, OUR FOUNDATION

IS BUILT ON _____. WE

VALUE _____ , _____ ,

AND _____. WE WILL ALWAYS

_____ BEFORE WE _____.

WE BELIEVE _____.

THERE'S NO ROOM FOR _____ HERE.

WE WILL ALWAYS FIGHT FOR _____

AND _____. EVEN ON OUR WORST

DAYS, WE _____ ,

AND _____ WILL ALWAYS

HOLD US TOGETHER.

**VALUES THAT ARE MOST
IMPORTANT TO MY FAMILY:**

**CAUSES AND ISSUES THAT
MATTER MOST TO MY FAMILY:**

**WAYS THAT WE GIVE
BACK AS A FAMILY:**

**WAYS THAT WE SUPPORT
EACH OTHER AS A FAMILY:**

MY DONATION PLANNER

WHOM I'M DONATING TO:

MOST REQUESTED OR NEEDED ITEMS:

SCHEDULED DROP-OFF DATE:

WHAT I WANT TO DONATE:

BEFORE DROP-OFF, ARE MY ITEMS:

- [ ] CLEAN OR FRESH?
- [ ] NEEDED OR REQUESTED ITEMS?
- [ ] NOT BROKEN OR DAMAGED?
- [ ] USABLE AND FUNCTIONAL?
- [ ] SOMETHING I'D WANT TO RECEIVE?

PEOPLE WHO CAN HELP ME:

STORES TO STOP BY:

NOTES:

How can you prioritize the dignity of the communities that you serve through your donations?

LET'S REFLECT

How can you create a rhythm of donating to people or organizations in need?

POLITICAL BINGO

From signing petitions to knowing who your elected representatives are, there are so many ways to stay politically engaged. Political decisions impact many aspects of our daily lives, both individually and collectively. Cross off every square that applies to your political engagement on the bingo board below and see if you can get four in a row.

VOTED IN A LOCAL ELECTION	SIGNED A PETITION	REGISTERED TO VOTE	SENT POST-CARDS TO VOTERS
ATTENDED A CITY COUNCIL MEETING	BEEN A POLL WORKER	KNOW THE NAME OF MY GOVERNOR	HELPED PEOPLE REGISTER TO VOTE
CONTACTED MY REPRESENTATIVE TO SHARE THOUGHTS	KNOW THE NAMES OF MY TWO SENATORS	VOTED IN A NATIONAL ELECTION	ATTENDED A PROTEST
DONATED TO A VOTING RIGHTS ORGANIZATION	PARTICIPATED IN PHONE BANKING	WATCHED A DEBATE	KNOW THE NAMES OF MY REPS

Is there anything on the bingo board that you haven't done yet but are willing to try?

Why does political engagement matter to you?

CONSIS

TENCY

MORNINGS AND EVENINGS

It's tempting to shy away from cultivating gentle rhythms because we're unable to execute them perfectly or aren't sure where to start. Thankfully, doing good daily doesn't require a flawless routine—just a posture of intentionality that helps you cultivate new habits. In this exercise, circle two ideas from each cloud that you're interested in adding to (or continuing to implement into) your morning or evening routine, and reflect on those choices on the next page.

IN THE MORNING

TAKING A
SHORT WALK

DRINKING A CUP
OF WATER

READING A FEW
PAGES OF A BOOK

WAITING BEFORE
SCROLLING THROUGH
SOCIAL MEDIA

JOURNALING

STRETCHING

READING ONE
NEWS STORY

MEDITATING ON A
QUOTE, SCRIPTURE, OR
TRUTH

THINKING OF A SIMPLE
GOOD DEED TO DO

LISTENING TO A
PODCAST EPISODE

IN THE EVENING 🌙

SPENDING TIME
WITH A HOBBY

DRINKING A CUP
OF WATER

ENDING PHONE USE
30 MINUTES BEFORE BED

REFLECTING ON
A MOMENT OF JOY
OR GRATITUDE

JOURNALING

STRETCHING

READING ONE
NEWS STORY

MEDITATING ON A
QUOTE, SCRIPTURE, OR
TRUTH

ORGANIZING ONE
SMALL AREA

LISTENING TO A
PODCAST EPISODE

Which rhythms did you select for your morning routine? What are the benefits of incorporating or continuing this rhythm?

Which rhythms did you select for your evening routine? What are the benefits of incorporating or continuing this rhythm?

LIVING IN ALIGNMENT

When living a life of dedication to our beliefs, there are moments when we have to sacrifice an opportunity, environment, or relationship to stay in alignment with our moral compass. In this activity, reflect on situations in your life where you had to walk away from something in order to keep your peace or integrity. After reflecting, give yourself an award for that decision. For example, a medal of bravery.

CERTIFICATE OF

_____

AWARDED TO

YOU

WHAT I HAD TO WALK AWAY FROM:

WHY I WALKED AWAY:

TROPHY OF:

_____

WHAT I HAD TO WALK AWAY FROM:

WHY I WALKED AWAY:

WHAT I HAD TO WALK AWAY FROM:

WHY I WALKED AWAY:

MEDAL OF:

_____

Why is it important to stick to your values, even when it could cost you something?

What is something that you gained or learned when you decided to live in alignment?

CARRYING WHAT I CAN

What issues, causes, or personal life burdens are you carrying right now?

Do you ever feel guilty for being unable to carry more of the world's troubles or take more action for causes you care about? Why or why not?

You are only one person and so much that goes on in the world is outside of your control. When you feel like you can't carry everything, what are things that you **can** do?

Taking action where we can helps to reduce feelings of helplessness. What's one small thing that you can do for someone else today?

THREE THINGS THAT ARE STILL TRUE ABOUT ME:

A LESSON I'VE LEARNED FROM THIS:

A MIND MAP FOR PROCESSING A MISTAKE

HOW THIS MISTAKE WILL CHANGE MY FUTURE DECISIONS FOR THE BETTER:

ONE INSPIRATIONAL QUOTE ABOUT MISTAKES THAT ENCOURAGES ME:

DO YOU STRUGGLE WITH FORGIVING YOURSELF AFTER A
MISTAKE? WHY OR WHY NOT?

HOW HAS SOMEONE ELSE'S TRANSPARENCY ABOUT THEIR OWN
MISTAKES HELPED YOU GROW?

THE BENEFITS OF REST

When I spend time doing this:

EX: PRACTICING MINDFULNESS AND MEDITATION

1

2

3

4

5

I can show up better for this:

EX: BEING MORE PATIENT WITH MY FAMILY

1

2

3

4

5

Reflect on how you approach rest. Do you feel like rest is something you have to earn? Why or why not?

What are the benefits, for you and for others, that come with being well-rested?

MY APPROACH TO SOCIAL MEDIA

THE SOCIAL NETWORKS I USE:

MY FAVORITE ACCOUNTS:

THE KINDS OF CONTENT I ENJOY:

I NEED A SOCIAL MEDIA BREAK WHEN I BEGIN TO FEEL:

MY SCROLLING TIME LIMIT:

HOW I WANT TO FEEL WHEN I'M USING SOCIAL MEDIA:

A TRUTH TO KEEP IN MIND WHILE USING SOCIAL MEDIA:

Do you ever struggle with doomscrolling or feeling like you have to consistently consume heavy content to stay informed? Why or why not?

Have you ever taken an extended social media break? What was that like for you? If not, would you consider it? Why or why not?

INNER ROADBLOCKS

In this activity, identify three roadblocks that may be preventing you from doing the good work that you were created for: things like fear of failure or self-doubt. Then, reflect on ways that you can work toward overcoming them.

ROADBLOCK 1:

HOW I CAN WORK TO OVERCOME IT:

ROADBLOCK 2:

HOW I CAN WORK TO OVERCOME IT:

ROADBLOCK 3:

HOW I CAN WORK TO OVERCOME IT:

What is something that you've always wanted to do that you've disqualified yourself from doing? Why did you decide not to do it?

Reflect on a time where you were underestimated or told that you couldn't achieve something and then went on to succeed. What did that experience teach you?

NAVIGATING BURNOUT

Have you ever experienced burnout? How did that show up for you?

What are the signs that you are at risk of burning out? These can be physical cues, mental health shifts, or other changes that take place.

Do you ever feel like you cannot afford to pause or rest? Why or why not?

Examine the toll that life has taken on your mind, body, and soul over the past few months. How are you doing? How can you make space for rest and recovery soon?

MY RHYTHM TRACKER

Do you have a rhythm you'd like to implement in your life on a daily, weekly, or monthly basis? This could be anything, from drinking more water to reading five pages a day. Keep track of your progress with the tracker below by identifying your goal and coloring in each "high five" as you complete your task.

MY GOAL: _____ 🖐 = _____

MY RHYTHM TRACKER

Do you have a rhythm you'd like to implement in your life on a daily, weekly, or monthly basis? This could be anything, from drinking more water to reading five pages a day. Keep track of your progress with the tracker below by identifying your goal and coloring in each flower as you complete your task.

MY GOAL: _____   FLOWER = _____

MY LITTLE JOYS

A major driver of consistency is finding joy in your journey. What brings you joy these days? What are small wins that you're proud of accomplishing? In the balloons below, make note of six things to celebrate or things that are making your days a bit brighter.

How do you celebrate your small wins? What new ideas could you implement in the future?

How can you make room for joy in the midst of challenging circumstances?

STRINGS OF CONNECTION

In this activity, reflect on something you're currently walking through, and then identify one way that you can find support or community with others who can relate to your burden or situation. Ideas include calling a friend, therapy, joining a support group, finding a book on the topic, etc.

SOMETHING I'M WALKING THROUGH:
Ex: Stress and a lack of direction.

A WAY TO FIND CONNECTION:
Ex: Reaching out to a mentor.

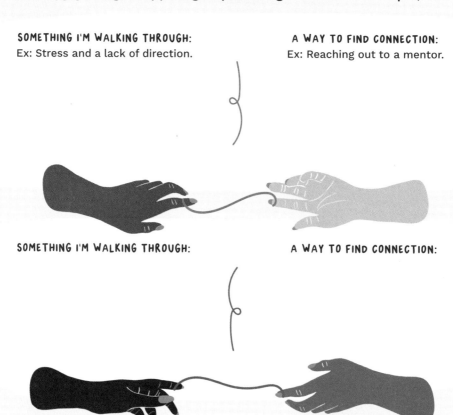

SOMETHING I'M WALKING THROUGH:

A WAY TO FIND CONNECTION:

SOMETHING I'M WALKING THROUGH:

A WAY TO FIND CONNECTION:

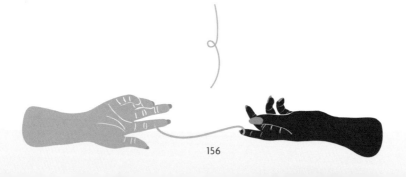

Is it challenging for you to ask for help or lean into community? Why or why not?

LET'S

REFLECT

Reflect on a time where you reached out to someone for connection and were strengthened or encouraged.

FIGHTING FALLACIES

Sometimes, our best efforts to empathize with others are interrupted by logical fallacies. These often show up as attempts by others (or even ourselves) to interrupt and invalidate the perspectives of others by bringing up irrelevant and distracting information, often derailing the moment into an argument. In this activity, you'll have an opportunity to research different kinds of fallacies and give examples of each so you're more aware of how they can show up in conversations.

STRAW MAN

Definition:

Example:

AD HOMINEM

Definition:

Example:

 **RED HERRING**

Definition:

Example:

 SLIPPERY SLOPE

Definition:

Example:

 WHATABOUTISM

Definition:

Example:

IT SHOULDN'T HAVE TO

HAPPEN TO YOU

FOR IT TO

MATTER TO YOU

How can you practice empathy without feeling like you have to absorb the weight all of the world's difficulties?

LET'S REFLECT

Why is it harmful to ignore issues taking place around the world?

SYMPATHY AND EMPATHY

While sympathy and empathy are both valuable and impactful practices that help others feel seen, empathy takes things a step further. In this activity, write down examples of showing sympathy and empathy for others and reflect on the differences between the two.

SYMPATHY

WISHES YOU WELL FOR THE JOURNEY AHEAD

Examples of showing sympathy:

Examples of showing empathy:

EMPATHY

COMES ALONG FOR THE CLIMB

How would you differentiate between sympathy and empathy? What do both have in common?

LET'S

REFLECT

What are some of the challenges or limitations that come with practicing empathy?

LEARNING SOMEONE'S STORY

When you have the capacity, create time to sit with someone else and hear their story. Listening and sharing stories grows our empathy, fosters connection, and gives us insight into differing perspectives.

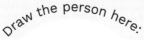 Draw the person here:

WHERE ARE THEY FROM? WHERE DO THEY LIVE?

WHAT BRINGS THEM JOY?

PEOPLE THEY LOVE:

WHAT CAUSES ARE THEY PASSIONATE ABOUT?

WHAT'S A DREAM THAT THEY HAVE?

FAVORITE SNACK:

FAVORITE COLOR:

WHAT'S ONE OF THEIR PET PEEVES?

FAVORITE PLACE:

How does sitting with someone else's story help us to increase our empathy?

Reflect on a time when learning a new part of someone else's story helped you to empathize with them on a deeper level.

PLANTING NEW RHYTHMS IN TENDER TIMES

Difficult seasons of global injustice or heartache often leave us tender. You may not know exactly what next step to take, but it's never a bad idea to be aware of this tenderness and find little ways to stay soft and open and dedicated to this good work in the midst of it. This activity will help you discover new rhythms to adopt during tough collective times and hopefully give you a glimmer of hope that change is still possible because it's happening within you.

	THE PLANTING	THE TENDING	THE SPROUTING
	SOWING NEW SEEDS	REGULAR RHYTHMS	GROWTH TO COME
EXAMPLE 1:	I WILL BECOME MORE AWARE OF GLOBAL NEWS.	• SOURCING UNBIASED, TRUTHFUL OUTLETS • SETTING ASIDE TIME TO TUNE IN REGULARLY • DISCOVERING A RHYTHM THAT WORKS BEST	A NEW AWARENESS OF WHAT'S TAKING PLACE IN THE WORLD AROUND US
EXAMPLE 2:			
EXAMPLE 3:			

166

How do you cope with global injustice or difficult news? Do you avoid it, process it with friends, journal about it, or something else?

How can you start to implement the ideas for new rhythms that you came up with on the previous page?

MY COMPASSION FATIGUE TOOLKIT

When leaning into empathy and compassion, it's critical to maintain outlets of self-expression, healing, and creativity to stay whole and well. In this activity, identify ways that you can incorporate or sustain hobbies, movement, meditative practices, and relaxation into your life regularly.

SOMETHING FUN:
(A hobby or exciting activity)

SOMETHING PHYSICAL:
(A way to move your body)

SOMETHING MEDITATIVE:
(A contemplative practice)

SOMETHING RESTORATIVE:
(A relaxing or refreshing activity)

Have you experienced compassion fatigue lately? What caused it? (Ex: The news cycle, social media comparison, being a caregiver, etc.)

Sometimes the weight of compassion requires community and walking through hardship with someone else. Is it hard for you to reach out to others for support? Whom can you lean on in difficult times? Consider putting together your toolkit with someone else or looping them into one of your four activities.

MY ENCOURAGEMENT ACTION PLAN

THE PERSON I WANT TO REACH OUT TO:

WHAT THIS PERSON IS GOING THROUGH:

WHEN I WANT TO REACH OUT:

IDEAS FOR AN ENCOURAGING TEXT:

A FEW OF THEIR FAVORITE THINGS:

IDEAS FOR AN INTENTIONAL
ACT OF KINDNESS:

SOMETHING TO TAKE OFF THEIR PLATE:

What kinds of words and actions have been most encouraging for you in difficult times? Can you recall a specific moment where someone showed up for you in a powerful way?

What are statements or actions to generally avoid when attempting to offer encouragement to someone else?

SAVIORISM VS. ACTIVISM

When we begin to center our own needs and efforts over the people we seek to support and empathize with, our activism can quickly morph into saviorism. In this activity, consider the thoughts given under the saviorism category and correct those thoughts in the activism category.

Saviorism says:

"I AM THE EXPERT AND KNOW WHAT'S BEST FOR THE COMMUNITY I'M SUPPORTING."

"THEY SHOULD BE GRATEFUL FOR WHATEVER I GIVE THEM."

"MY THOUGHTS, FEELINGS, AND PREFERENCES ARE AT THE CENTER."

"I AM ABOVE THE PEOPLE I AM SUPPORTING."

"IT'S MY JOB TO FIX EVERYTHING."

"IF I DON'T DO THIS, NOBODY ELSE WILL."

Activism says:

EX: "MY ACTIONS SUPPORT THE LOCAL COMMUNITY AND ORGANIZATIONS ALREADY ON THE GROUND."

Has there been a time where you operated as a savior for another person or community? Reflect on that experience.

What are practical ways that you can prevent your good intentions from morphing into saviorism when doing activism work?

REFLECTING ON ACTIVE LISTENING

How would you describe a thoughtful listener?

Describe a time where you were sharing something with someone else but you did not feel heard or cared for during that conversation. What specific actions, or lack thereof, caused you to feel this way?

Describe a time where you fell short as an active listener during a conversation with someone else. What happened, and what would you do differently today?

What role does active and empathetic listening play during seasons of hardship?

THE LIGHT OF TRUTH

A lie that society wants me to believe:

1   EX: THE ABSENT BLACK FATHER MYTH

2

3

4

5

The truth that I'm clinging to:

1   EX: RESEARCH FROM THE CDC FOUND THAT BLACK FATHERS ARE MORE INVOLVED IN THEIR CHILDREN'S LIVES COMPARED TO OTHER RACIAL GROUPS

2

3

4

5

Why do opponents of justice often push "fake news," "alternative facts," or lies?

How can you prioritize truth-telling in your advocacy and justice work?

SIGNS TO PAY ATTENTION TO

Doing the work of changemaking often involves difficult conversations, introspection, and unlearning. It's easy to underestimate the toll that this can have on our minds and emotions. Are you aware of the internal or external signs that may point to a need to slow down, stop, or change directions? This activity will help you reflect on the the signals your body may be giving you when it's time to make a change for the sake of your mental and emotional health on your journey.

I KNOW I NEED TO CHANGE DIRECTIONS WHEN:
(Ex: I'm feeling misaligned with the cause)

I KNOW I SHOULD SLOW DOWN WHEN:
(Ex: I'm experiencing overwhelm)

I KNOW I SHOULD STOP OR TAKE A BREAK WHEN:
(Ex: I'm burning out or having panic attacks)

Do you find it difficult to listen to your body and slow down or stop?

Having uncomfortable conversations does not mean that you need to open yourself up to harm or attack. What are your boundaries when engaging in heated conversations?

MY TOUGH CONVERSATION PLANNER

I NEED TO HAVE A TALK WITH:

GOAL OF THIS CONVERSATION:

DATE AND TIME TO MAKE IT HAPPEN:

KEY POINTS TO COVER;

MY FEEDBACK SANDWICH:

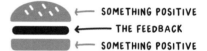

← SOMETHING POSITIVE

← THE FEEDBACK

← SOMETHING POSITIVE

:

:

:

MY POST—TALK SELF CARE WILL BE:

I CAN PRACTICE THIS TALK WITH:

Do you find it hard to speak your mind and have tough conversations? Why or why not?

Which causes more inner turmoil for you: the discomfort that comes with speaking your mind or the discomfort that comes with holding back to keep the peace? Why?

CONNECTING THE DOTS OF HISTORY

History helps to explain how we got here, and why things are the way that they are. Connecting the dots between then and now helps us to see what work still needs to be done and trace issues to their root causes. In this activity, you'll get to connect the dots between present-day issues and their origins. You can connect each issue to as many causes as you'd like. When you're finished, you'll have a tangled web between history and the present, illuminating the need we have as a society to continue dismantling harmful systems.

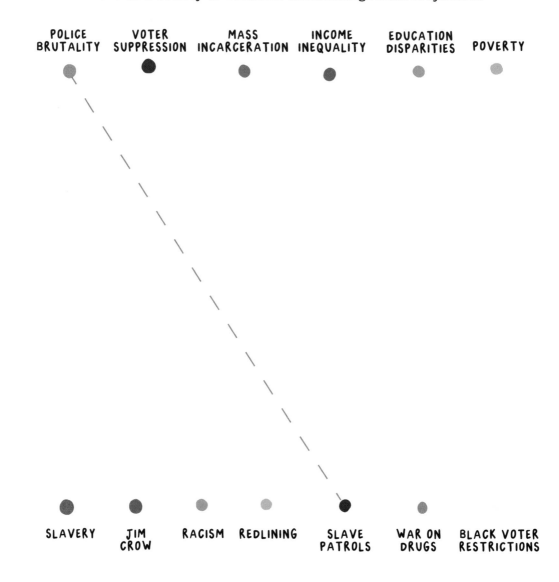

POLICE BRUTALITY VOTER SUPPRESSION MASS INCARCERATION INCOME INEQUALITY EDUCATION DISPARITIES POVERTY

SLAVERY JIM CROW RACISM REDLINING SLAVE PATROLS WAR ON DRUGS BLACK VOTER RESTRICTIONS

Why is it important that we continue making
connections between the past and present?

How can you incorporate memory and history into your present-day
advocacy and justice work?

MY TOP THREE NEWS SOURCES

Being intentional about the news sources we use can help us guard against misinformation and prevent information overload. In this activity, choose three sources that you can keep on rotation and describe how you'll engage with them.

NAME: _____

Circle the source type:

PODCAST   PUBLICATION   WEBSITE   VIDEO OR TV

WHY I CHOSE THIS SOURCE:

HOW OFTEN I'LL ENGAGE WITH IT:

NAME: _____

Circle the source type:

PODCAST   PUBLICATION   WEBSITE   VIDEO OR TV

WHY I CHOSE THIS SOURCE:

HOW OFTEN I'LL ENGAGE WITH IT:

NAME: _____

Circle the source type:

PODCAST   PUBLICATION   WEBSITE   VIDEO OR TV

WHY I CHOSE THIS SOURCE:

HOW OFTEN I'LL ENGAGE WITH IT:

If one of your news sources is a major news publication, look it up on a media bias rating website. How biased is your news source?

Read or listen to a news story and try to trace back to one of the original, or primary, source(s) that are referenced in it. You can do this by clicking included links, looking up the sources mentioned, reading firsthand accounts, or analyzing the provided data. What did you discover? Was the story misleading or true to its headline?

UNPOPULAR OPINIONS

Do you hold any positions or values that deeply matter to you but may be seen as unpopular to others? In this activity, reflect on three of your unpopular opinions and explain why you hold those beliefs.

UNPOPULAR OPINION 1:

_____
_____
_____
_____
_____
_____
_____

_____
_____
_____
_____
_____
_____
_____
_____

UNPOPULAR OPINION 2:

UNPOPULAR OPINION 3:

_____
_____
_____
_____
_____
_____
_____
_____

Do you find it difficult to express or defend your unpopular opinions? Why or why not?

What are the dangers of only doing the work when it's a trending topic?

THINGS I WON'T APOLOGIZE FOR

In this activity, you'll get a chance to identify ways that you've been taught to shrink or minimize yourself. Changing for the better is always good, but there are times when criticism or negative feedback can cause us to dislike things about ourselves that make us who we are. What core personality traits or passions have you been told to discard, and how can you gently reclaim them?

I'll no longer apologize for:
EX: MY LOUD LAUGH

I'll reclaim this by:
EX: NOT HOLDING BACK MY JOY

I'll no longer apologize for:

I'll reclaim this by:

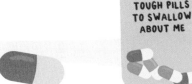

TOUGH PILLS
TO SWALLOW
ABOUT ME

I'll no longer apologize for:

I'll no longer apologize for:

I'll reclaim this by:

I'll reclaim this by:

When it comes to being your authentic self, are you more likely to shrink back or shine brightly? Why?

What affirmations can you repeat to yourself when you feel tempted to dim your light?

MY BRIDGE TO BOLDNESS

Boldness bridges the gap between good intentions and good work, and crossing that bridge will require preparation. In the spaces below, reflect on what steps you need to take to live a life of boldness and how you'll avoid the dangers of fear and comparison.

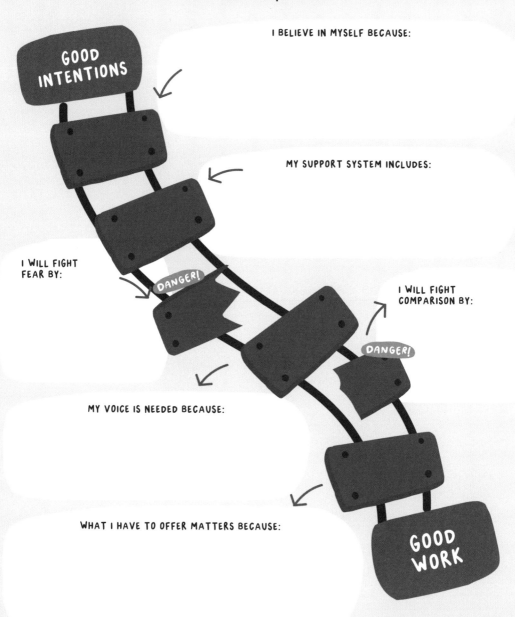

GOOD INTENTIONS

I BELIEVE IN MYSELF BECAUSE:

MY SUPPORT SYSTEM INCLUDES:

I WILL FIGHT FEAR BY:

DANGER!

I WILL FIGHT COMPARISON BY:

DANGER!

MY VOICE IS NEEDED BECAUSE:

WHAT I HAVE TO OFFER MATTERS BECAUSE:

GOOD WORK

Reflect on a time when comparison, fear, or self-doubt held you back from doing something and describe what that experience was like.

Reflect on a time when you were bold and took a chance on doing something and describe what that experience was like.

What is virtue signaling? How does virtue signaling fuel performative activism?

What pressures, external or internal, often lead people into performative activism?

Reflect on a time where you engaged in performative activism or witnessed someone else doing it. What happened, and what did you take away from it?

What are the broader implications of performative activism? How can it negatively affect a movement?

How can you practice being gentle with yourself?
Which areas of your life can benefit from a bit
more self-compassion?

How have you grown over the past year? How can you celebrate that
growth?

REDEM

PTION

Calling In

mobile

COMPLIMENT CONFETTI!!

On each piece of confetti, write one thing that you like about yourself, something you've overcome, or a reason why you're proud of yourself.

1.

2.

3.

4.

5.

6.

7.

8.

9.

10.

Why is it important to prioritize restorative justice over retributive justice?

How do you practice restoration and redemption in your own relationships?

REFLECTING ON FORGIVENESS

Is there someone in your life whom you need to forgive? Who is it, and what happened?

Have you felt burdened by the weight of unforgiveness at a point in your life? What was that experience like?

Is there anything that you need to forgive yourself for? If so, what is it?

What are some possible positive outcomes that you can experience when you forgive yourself and/or others?

LAYING MY CARDS ON THE TABLE

When seeking to practice redemption with others, it's helpful to have clarity with our own needs, desires, and boundaries. When we're clear about what's important for ourselves, it's easier to lay our cards on the table and communicate those matters to others with clarity. Respond to the prompts on the cards below with answers that reflect the truest version of you.

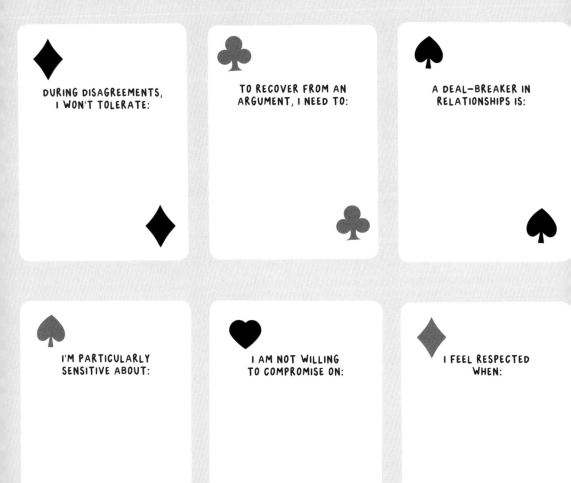

♦ DURING DISAGREEMENTS, I WON'T TOLERATE:

♣ TO RECOVER FROM AN ARGUMENT, I NEED TO:

♠ A DEAL-BREAKER IN RELATIONSHIPS IS:

♠ I'M PARTICULARLY SENSITIVE ABOUT:

♥ I AM NOT WILLING TO COMPROMISE ON:

♦ I FEEL RESPECTED WHEN:

How can having clarity about your own boundaries and needs help you navigate difficult conversations or situations?

How do you honor the dignity of the other party in the midst of a disagreement?

REFLECTING ON REPARATIONS

What are your thoughts on reparations in general?

Describe a time in world history where a reparations program was attempted. Who was supposed to receive reparations? Was the program successful or unsuccessful?

If a reparations program were to be introduced this year, what should be included? What would it look like? Who would receive reparations?

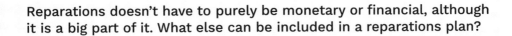

Reparations doesn't have to purely be monetary or financial, although it is a big part of it. What else can be included in a reparations plan?

CALLING OUT

Recall a time where you were called out for harmful behavior. How did that affect you? What lesson did you learn?

Recall a time where you had to call someone else out for harmful behavior. What did you take away from that experience?

CALLING IN

Have you ever used "calling in" as an alternative to "calling out" harmful behavior? How did it go? In what instances would you call in as opposed to call out?

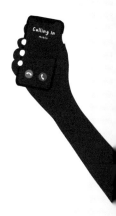

Do you view "calling in" as an adequate alternative to "calling out" in certain instances? Why or why not?

WHAT DOES IT MEAN TO "DO JUSTICE"?   HOW CAN YOU DO JUSTICE IN LIFE?

WHAT DOES IT MEAN TO "LOVE MERCY"?   HOW CAN YOU LOVE MERCY IN LIFE?

WHAT DOES IT MEAN TO "WALK HUMBLY"?   HOW CAN YOU WALK HUMBLY IN LIFE?

Many people who are passionate about doing justice can trace this value back to an event or incident that spurred them into action. What's yours? If yours wasn't a specific event, why do you value doing justice?

LET'S

REFLECT

What role does mercy play in justice work?

MY APOLOGY PLANNER

WHOM I'D LIKE TO APOLOGIZE TO:

WHY I'M APOLOGIZING:

A RECAP OF THE SITUATION:

HOW I'LL CHANGE MY BEHAVIOR
MOVING FORWARD:

DO I WANT TO KEEP
WORKING ON THIS   YES   NO
RELATIONSHIP?

WHY OR WHY NOT?

Do you find it hard to apologize or take accountability? Why or why not?

Is there a time where you've had to end a relationship, even when an apology was offered? What did you take away from that experience?

REDEMPTION THROUGHOUT HISTORY

History is filled with examples of wrong being made right. While the impacts of harmful systems are long-lasting, we can find hope in the fact that we have evidence of reformed policies and corrective measures that seek to make amends and begin the work of redemption. In this activity, list an example of a corrective measure taken, by the government or other organizations, to change the harmful laws, practices, or systems listed below, then describe if additional work needs to be done.

SLAVERY

Corrective measures taken:

Additional work to do:

VOTING RIGHTS

Corrective measures taken:

Additional work to do:

THE WAR ON DRUGS

Corrective measures taken:

Additional work to do:

SEGREGATION

Corrective measures taken:

Additional work to do:

In the spaces below, identify your own examples of wrongs committed by the government, society at large, or people in your own life. Then describe ways that they attempted to make things right, and if work still needs to be done.

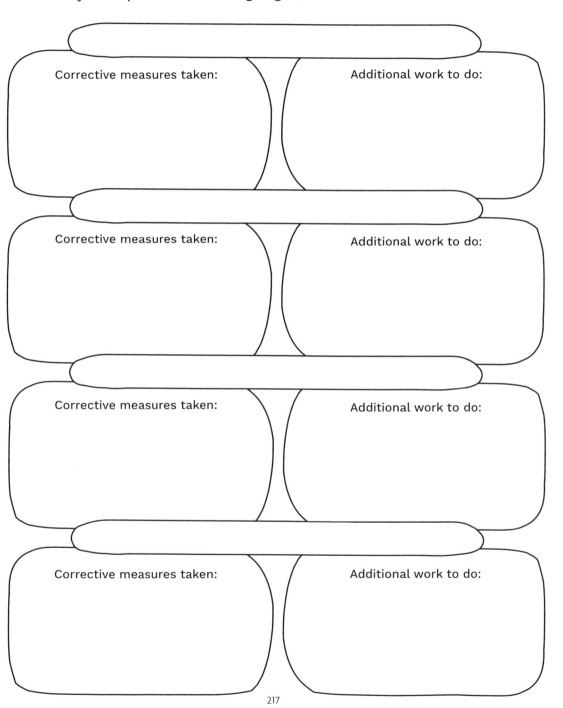

Corrective measures taken:

Additional work to do:

Corrective measures taken:

Additional work to do:

Corrective measures taken:

Additional work to do:

Corrective measures taken:

Additional work to do:

THE FRUIT OF CHANGE

When my heart changed about this:

1 EX: RELEASING PERFECTIONISM AND THE NEED TO NEVER MAKE MISTAKES

2

3

4

5

My actions changed by:

1 EX: GIVING MORE GRACE TO MYSELF AND MY IMPERFECTIONS

2

3

4

5

Describe one of the heart changes you wrote about in the last activity in more detail. What was this transformation like?

Reflect on a time when people around you noticed a positive change in you. What did they say about it? What is the evidence of transformation for the better in your life?

SOLUTION KEY

COME TOGETHER CROSSWORD

SOLUTION PAGE 10

Across

1. recycling
7. review
8. organization
9. community
10. compliment
11. donation
13. thrifting
14. shelter

Down

2. generosity
3. note
4. meal train
5. petition
6. volunteering
12. tutoring
14. small

WORD SEARCH SOUP

SOLUTION PAGE 34

```
N K Z X P G G X T K N G E V B V U L U
Z O V R N K U J V V J T D O R E O I E
M W I F U S S P I A T Y R I J X Z P Q
T A L E N T S K H F J J X C I U P A I
L Z T S U R I Q Z R B M P E S Z E S R
D R X C O M M U N I T Y U H B T G S J
M V I S I O N P V N L L V K K S W I P
G W G A H X V C J G Y D W X O M L O N
U H O S W C J O U Q J N C S V G I N R
E J R T G P D R S C U L T U R E L S S
I Q A Y V N J G T E V Q A V G L U R Q
V Q S L Y Z K W O U J L B I L W E F W
D H I E D F K D R I Z N M S O X E K I
N A O M T P B Q Y W O E E Z K T P V A
O C T B N U J E T I H P V U D I Q G Q
R U J T B B C B Z A J L U W X X L A P
L J Z P S I S M Q A R Q A F Y I U L M
P D H Z V M E P Y M R O B D F S L Q S
Z D X B P P R S M Y F X L T N T L L Y
```

222

SONGS OF FREEDOM

SOLUTION PAGE 78

SWING LOW SWEET CHARIOT

FOLLOW THE DRINKING GOURD

WADE IN THE WATER

STEAL AWAY

GO DOWN MOSES

WE SHALL OVERCOME

OH FREEDOM

DOWN BY THE RIVERSIDE

HOW I GOT OVER

ABOUT THE AUTHOR

Danielle Coke Balfour is a designer turned illustrator, advocate, speaker, entrepreneur, and author. She's the founder of Oh Happy Dani—a lifestyle brand and educational platform that uses artwork and resources to encourage empathy, inspire justice, and make complex ideas more accessible—and her first book, *A Heart on Fire: 100 Meditations on Loving Your Neighbors Well*, published in the fall of 2023. Danielle is driven by her desire to help everyday advocates do good daily in their spheres of influence using their passions and skills, and she's fostered a community of over half a million people who share her vision across social media. With a joy that flows from her desire to love her neighbor as herself, Danielle hopes to spark action toward a pursuit of the ultimate good as you hold her art in your home and carry it in your heart.

Andrews McMeel Publishing
a division of Andrews McMeel Universal
1130 Walnut Street, Kansas City, Missouri 64106

www.andrewsmcmeel.com

24 25 26 27 28 SDB 10 9 8 7 6 5 4 3 2 1

ISBN: 978-1-5248-8821-3

Editor: Patty Rice
Art Director/Designer: Tiffany Meairs
Production Editor: David Shaw
Production Manager: Tamara Haus

ATTENTION: SCHOOLS AND BUSINESSES

Andrews McMeel books are available at quantity discounts with bulk purchase for educational, business, or sales promotional use. For information, please e-mail the Andrews McMeel Publishing Special Sales Department: sales@amuniversal.com.